THEN & NOW

KENT COUNTY

OPPOSITE: The Caulk's Field Monument was erected in 1902 to "commemorate the patriotism and fortitude of the victor and vanquished." The monument recognizes the battle fought by the Kent County militia under Lt. Col. Philip A. Reed. The Kent County militia marched from Belle Air (now the town Fairlee) to meet British forces here on August 31, 1814. With the loss of 15 men, as well as their commander, Sir Peter Parker, the British were defeated. American losses were slight. (Courtesy of the Historical Society of Kent County.)

THEN & NOW

KENT COUNTY

William A. "Pat" Biddle,
Patricia Joan O. Horsey,
and R. Jerry Keiser

ISBN 978-0-7385-8672-4

Library of Congress Control Number: 2010928167

Published by Arcadia Publishing
Charleston, South Carolina

Printed in the United States of America

For all general information, please contact Arcadia Publishing:
Telephone 843-853-2070
Fax 843-853-0044
E-mail sales@arcadiapublishing.com
For customer service and orders:
Toll-Free 1-888-313-2665

Visit us on the Internet at www.arcadiapublishing.com

On the Front Cover: Radcliffe Driving Park, also known as Chestertown Driving Park and Stepney Race Track, is located on Quaker Neck Road on the edge of Chestertown. It was the site of horse racing at the turn of the century. On May 31, 1915, on "Decoration Day," local residents enjoyed "Mutuel Races" at Radcliffe Park, where the horses "were called to the wire" at 2:00 p.m. The property where the racetrack is located has been sold for development. (Courtesy of the Historical Society of Kent County.)

On the Back Cover: Middle, East, and West Halls are located on the Washington College campus in Chestertown. They stand on the crest of a low hill (the terrace) at the center of the campus. Middle Hall was built in 1844 and the East and West Halls were built in 1854. They are the oldest surviving campus buildings. They serve as monuments to the original Common Building (completed in 1789), the site of which they occupy. They are all three-story buildings constructed of brick and are used as dormitories today. (Courtesy of the Historical Society of Kent County.)

Contents

Acknowledgments

We would like to thank the following people for their help and cooperation in providing the photographs and post cards for this book: Austin Walmsley, photographer; Heather Davidson, photographer; Barbara B. Heck, associate vice president for leadership gifts, Washington College; Diane Daniels and Joan Andersen of the Historical Society of Kent County; H. Edward Beekman Jr.; the William B. Usilton family for sharing their photograph collection of local landmarks and events with the Historical Society of Kent County; the Maryland Historical Society; Kevin Hemstock; Mary Anna Gustafson; Karen Collier; Edgar Glenn; Robin Wood Kurowski; Judy Hickman; Todd B. Smith; Scott O. Smith; Tracye S. Landon; and all who generously shared their vintage photographs for this book.

All author proceeds from the sale of this book will go to the Kent County Public Library.

We'd like to acknowledge the following for their special support: Elmer E. Horsey, James Thomas (J. T.) Ozman Landon, Frank Ozman Smith, Kathryn Macey Smith, Carli Crew Smith, Baker Fallon Horsey Landon, Jennifer Ashley Horsey, Lauren Nicholson Horsey, Barbara and Glen Biddle, Gabriela, Claudia, and Nathan Biddle, and Jacob and Evelyn Keiser.

All modern images are courtesy of the authors.

Introduction

In their makeshift shallop, Capt. John Smith and his crew entered the Sassafras River in the late summer of 1608. Today the Sassafras River forms the northern boundary of Kent County, Maryland. Smith originally called the river Tockwough after the Native Americans who lived on the southern banks of the river. Smith's crew skirted the coastline of Kent County to the mouth of the Chester River before crossing the Chesapeake Bay to the western shore on their journey back south to Jamestown. In one of the most famous images of America, Smith's 1612 Map of Virginia, Kent County is shown with the name Tockwough over what is the Kent County peninsula today.

Kent County, named for Kent County in England, was officially founded in 1642, about 34 years after John Smith discovered and explored its northern boundary. On Kent's southern boundary is the Chester River, a river that also meanders its way to the Chesapeake Bay. On the banks of this river, the town of Newtown (later named Chestertown) was founded.

Chestertown was designated as the port of entry for the northern counties of Cecil, Kent, and Queen Anne's Counties. Founded in 1706, Chestertown is the largest town in Kent County and is the county seat. Chestertown has maintained most of its 18th-century architecture and history, both of which are on display every Memorial Day weekend for the Chestertown Tea Party. This annual event commemorates the boarding of the brigantine *Geddes*, anchored in the Chester River on May 23, 1774. A group of citizens tossed the *Geddes* cargo of tea into the Chester River in response to the closing of the Port of Boston.

In addition to dissenting against Great Britain's colonial policies, Chestertown and Kent County contributed men, arms, and food to the Revolutionary War effort. Kent County was the most vital source on the Eastern Shore for armaments, and the war contributions from the area's farmers and millers led the area to be called the "bread basket of the revolution." Finally, at the war's end, Col. Tench Tilghman carried the news of Cornwallis's surrender at Yorktown on horseback through the Kent County countryside to Philadelphia.

With the war over, the citizens of Kent County returned to their farms, mercantile affairs, and to the proper education of their young men. It was in Kent County, in the town of Chestertown, that

Washington College was founded in 1782. The institution has been a significant part of Kent County and the nation's history, as it was the first college founded in the United States of America. Named for George Washington, it was the only college to receive his "expressed consent" for the naming. In addition, he donated funds to its founding. Throughout his life, Washington's connection with the school became a source of historical pride for the county residents.

It did not take Britain long to forget its experience with its former colonies, and especially those colonists located in Kent County. The British had been burning towns, such as Georgetown, at the mouth of the Sassafras River, during the summer of 1814. However, on August 31, 1814, in what was undoubtedly the turning point in the War of 1812, the Battle of Caulk's Field took place in Kent County. It was here that Col. Phillip Read and his 174 militiamen fought and defeated a force of over 200 British troops and marines on the battlefield. On September 12, 1814, the Boston *Independent Chronicle* declared the excellent news in four words: "Huzza for the Militia."

Kent County's towns and villages continued to play an important role in Maryland and United States history: Mason and Dixon would spend time surveying the boundary line between Maryland and Delaware, the Civil War would claim 400 members of our society on both sides, thousands would come to play at our beaches at Betterton and Tolchester, and women would vote before the 19th Amendment. It is our hope that this photographic narrative will provide a glimpse into the cultural panorama of Kent County, and that you will discover, as did John Smith and his fellow explorers, that Kent County is a great place to visit and experience history.

CHAPTER 1

CHESTERTOWN

This photograph of the Chestertown Fair was taken around 1915. The fair was held at Radcliffe Driving Park on Quaker Neck Road, just outside of Chestertown. The banner is advertising the Chestertown Candy Kitchen, which was located where Chesapeake Bank stands today. The fair was usually held in May. There was a baseball game and horse races. Admission to the game and races was 25¢. (Courtesy of Historical Society of Kent County.)

The Chestertown Armory was added to the National Register of Historic Places in 1985. It was built in 1931 for Company G, 115th Battalion of the 29th Division of the Maryland National Guard. The Armory has been used for a number of community events over the years, including dances, bazaars, fund-raising events, and even Washington College basketball games. The building is no longer used by the Maryland National Guard. A World War II National Guard Medical Detachment monument remains on the property. (Courtesy of William A. "Pat" Biddle.)

The Chestertown High School building, located on Washington Avenue in Chestertown, was built in 1915. The costs were $3,700 for the lot and $16,800 for the building. Additions were added to the original center structure. The building is currently being used as the offices of the Kent County Board of Education. In 2010, The Kent County Commissioners decided to sell the building. That same year, the Kent County Board of Education announced it would be moving to the former Rock Hall Elementary School building. (Courtesy of William A. "Pat" Biddle.)

The first public library for Kent County was located on Court Street in downtown Chestertown. It served the community from January 2, 1962, until September 1, 1962. It was relocated to the "Bartley Building" on High Street, and then moved to a new building on High Street, where it remains today. In 2003 an annex building, the Chestertown Library Inc. building directly behind the library, was remodeled for its use. (Photograph courtesy of Karen Collier.)

This building, located at 400 High Street in Chestertown, once served as a high school. It later became the Chestertown Elementary School, with grades one through six. The original cupola on the stair tower was removed in 1956. The building was restored and an addition was added to the rear. Today it serves as the Kent County Government office building. (Courtesy of William A. "Pat" Biddle.)

Fountain Park is located in the heart of downtown Chestertown. It was a project of the Ladies Improvement Association and was dedicated in 1899. Hebe, the goddess of youth and beauty, as well as the "cupbearer to the gods," stands atop the ornate cast-iron fountain. The Chestertown Garden Club donated concrete and wooden benches for Fountain Park in honor of Chestertown's 250th anniversary. Brick sidewalks leading to the fountain were completed and dedicated in 1984. (Courtesy of William A. "Pat" Biddle.)

Pictured above are members attending a Masonic meeting at Jane's Church in 1940 in Chestertown. The original Jane's United Methodist Church, built around 1866 by John T. Dodd, was destroyed by fire in March 1914. The building was owned by L. Bates Russell. A new Jane's Methodist Memorial Church, located at the corner of Cross and Cannon Streets, was dedicated in November 1914. (Courtesy of the Historical Society of Kent County.)

The Kent and Queen Anne's Hospital (now Chester River Hospital Center) had its beginnings on High Street in Chestertown. In 1933, construction began to build a new hospital on an 8-acre parcel in Chestertown. The hospital was renamed Chester River Hospital Center in July 2003 and merged with the University of Maryland Medical System in 2009. It celebrated its 75th anniversary in 2010. (Courtesy of the Historical Society of Kent County.)

The White Swan Tavern is located on High Street in downtown Chestertown. In 1733, Joseph Nicholson built it as a residence on Chestertown's lot No. 76 (original plat). The property was formerly used as a tannery operated by a Chestertown shoemaker, John Lovegrove. The building was restored to its 1796 appearance in the late 1970s and reopened in 1981 as a bed and breakfast. (Courtesy of the Historical Society of Kent County.)

Metcalfe Brothers Grain and Feed Company, located in Chestertown, was founded after World War I by brothers "Brownie" and "Jimmy" Metcalfe. It operated at the Cross Street extended location until the 1950s when the business was moved to Price's Station in nearby Queen Anne's County. The building today houses a doctor's office, a beauty salon, and a conference center. (Courtesy of Gwinn Derricott.)

The above photograph of Shore Radio and Auto Supply, which was located on Cross Street in downtown Chestertown, was taken in the 1950s. It was owned by the late Phil Kratzer. Over the years, the building has also been used as a beauty shop and children's shop. Today it is The Village House, a retail shop that offers a unique mix of classic interiors and timeless accessories. (Courtesy of the Historical Society of Kent County.)

This four-corner area of downtown Chestertown, commonly referred to as "Bordley's Corner," is located at the meeting of Cross Street and High Street. Thomas S. Bordley operated a gentlemen's goods and clothing store in the corner building shown in 1877. It was destroyed by fire in 1910 and rebuilt in 1911. The men's haberdashery store descended in the Bordley family until it closed in 1950. The Bordley family continues to own the building, which they currently lease. (Courtesy of the Historical Society of Kent County.)

The hook-and-ladder engine below, converted from a Pierce Arrow touring car, was proudly displayed at the Fourth of July parade in Chestertown by the Chestertown Volunteer Fire Company in 1925. Today the Chestertown Volunteer Fire Company has a 2004 tanker with a capacity of 4,000 gallons, a 1989 ladder truck with a 100 foot ladder (above), a 2008 brush truck, a 1995 rescue truck, and three engines. (Courtesy of the Historical Society of Kent County and Patricia Joan O. Horsey.)

The Kent County Court House is located in downtown Chestertown. The first courthouse, built in 1707, was partially destroyed by fire in 1719 and the replacement, constructed in 1720, was renovated in 1750. That courthouse was torn down in 1860, so a new one could be built in the current Italianate style. This building was enlarged in 1912 and again in 1937. In 1969, a new Colonial-style addition was constructed, with an entrance facing Cross Street. The building remains in this location today. (Courtesy of William A. "Pat" Biddle.)

This building, once located just outside of the present Court House on Cross Street in Chestertown, was formerly the Kent County Magistrate's Building. In 1988, it was moved to its present location at 333 South Cross Street to be renovated into the current Chestertown Police Department building. (Courtesy of the Horsey Collection.)

The interior of Stam Drugs is illustrated above as it was in 1877, when it was located in Stam Hall on High Street in downtown Chestertown. The store, owned by Colin F. Stam, was later moved across the street to its present location. The soda fountain in today's Stam Drug Store was purchased used and installed in 1935. (Courtesy of the Historical Society of Kent County.)

This view of Cannon Street in Chestertown is looking toward the Chester River. Cannon Street has experienced a dramatic redevelopment in the last 20 years. Chestertown rose in stature when it was named one of Maryland's six Royal Ports of Entry. A shipping boom followed this designation, making the town at the navigable head of the Chester River wealthy. In the mid-eighteenth century, Chestertown was considered Maryland's second leading port, with Annapolis being number one. (Courtesy of the Horsey Collection.)

The Voshell House opened in 1864 and dominated the corner of High and Spring Streets in Chestertown for many years. The Peoples Bank, established on April 13, 1910, bought the building in 1962 and demolished it to make room for the building that exists today. The Peoples Bank celebrated 100 years of "Peoples" serving people in 2010. (Courtesy of the Historical Society of Kent County.)

HIGH STREET AND VOSHELL HOUSE, CHESTERTOWN, MD.

The Maryland General Assembly granted this lot in Chestertown to the Masons in 1826. The Masons had a hall on the second floor. It is believed the Masons remained in this location until a local newspaper company arrived in 1849. This building, known as the Kent News Building for many years, is now the Hogans Building. (Courtesy of the Historical Society of Kent County.)

The Chestertown Railroad Station was built in 1902–1903 by W. S. Culp and A. M. Culp for $4,000. Western Union selected this station as the site for its telegraph office when telegraph service was first brought to Kent County at the opening of the station on June 1, 1903. In 1981, the station was moved approximately 44 feet to the north, so that Cross Street could be extended. (Courtesy of the Historical Society of Kent County.)

Bill Bennett's Service Station and Luncheonette was located on Washington Avenue in Chestertown at the edge of the Washington College campus. It served the community as the Trailways Bus Station in 1945 and was a gathering place for high school and Washington College students for many years. Today the site is home to a Rita's franchise, which offers "Ice – Custard – Happiness." (Courtesy of William F. "Bill" Bennett.)

The front two-story section of Eliason Motors, built in the late 1800s on Cross Street in downtown Chestertown, was once the Armstrong Hotel. In 1923, The Eliason family bought the building and opened their business, Eliason Motors. The company sold Ford cars, trucks, and tractors from 1923 until 1975. Fire destroyed the building in 1991. Today it remains a vacant lot next to the Chestertown Town Hall. (Courtesy of the Historical Society of Kent County.)

Historic Widehall is located on Chestertown's waterfront. Built in 1769 by Thomas Smyth, it later was the home of Robert Wright, governor of Maryland from 1806 to 1809; and of Ezekiel F. Chambers, state and U.S. senator and judge of the Court of Appeals. It was listed on the National Register of Historic Places in 1972 and is a contributing property in the Chestertown Historic District. The name "Widehall" comes from the size of the second story hall. (Courtesy William A. "Pat" Biddle.)

Wilbur W. Hubbard built The Imperial Hotel (on the right) on High Street in Chestertown in 1903. The building to its left is now the Prince Theatre. Over the years, the Imperial was converted into offices and apartments, and in the 1970s, it was partially renovated to house six small ground-level shops. It was restored as a hotel in 1986 and today offers lodging and dining. (Courtesy of the Historical Society of Kent County.)

The Chestertown Seventh Day Adventist Church is located on Kent Street in Chestertown. In 1943 at the Chestertown Fire Hall, a series of meetings were held for those interested in establishing a Seventh Day Adventist church in Chestertown. It was built in 1945. The church remains active in the community today. (Courtesy of the Historical Society of Kent County.)

The Samuel Vannort House was built in 1887 at 350 High Street in Chestertown, next to the First Methodist Church. It was torn down in 1949 and a new structure was built. The new building was first occupied by the Acme Market and later by Bonnett's Department Store, a retail clothing shop for men and women. Today the building contains the offices of the Kent County Department of Social Services. (Courtesy of the Savage family.)

This building, located in downtown Chestertown on High Street, was once Schreiber's Wholesale and Retail Confectionery. It was opened in 1918 by Charles C. Schreiber. The building has been restored and is now home to Brix Tapas Kitchen and Wine Cellar. (Courtesy of the Schreiber family.)

This was the interior of Schreiber's Wholesale and Retail Confectionery on High Street in downtown Chestertown. Schreiber's sold newspapers, school supplies, penny candy, ice cream, and many other items. Today the building is home to Brix Tapas Kitchen and Wine Cellar. (Courtesy of the Schreiber family.)

108 South Cross Street in downtown Chestertown was once Loud's Ice Cream Parlor, followed in 1919 by Gill Brothers Ice Cream and Milk. The young people of the 1900s enjoyed the dance floor and the booths in the basement of the building before it became Woodie's restaurant. Following its restaurant days, it was The Sly Horse, a retail clothing and gift shop, followed by a kitchen shop. Today it houses Play It Again Sam's, a coffeehouse with a wine bar. (Courtesy of the Historical Society of Kent County.)

The former location of Mutual Fire Insurance of Kent County, Maryland, on High Street in Chestertown, is now a part of PNC Bank (previously The Chestertown Bank of Maryland). The Mutual Fire Insurance Company moved from this location to a building next door, where an insurance agency still operates today. (Courtesy of the Historical Society of Kent County.)

Emmanuel Episcopal Church is located in the heart of Chestertown's historic district. The land was granted for the building in 1768 by the Provincial Council from the Court House lands. The original structure was erected between 1768 and 1772 as a chapel of ease in then-new Chester Parish. It was the site of the convention that proposed and adopted the name "Protestant Episcopal Church" in 1780. (Courtesy of William A. "Pat" Biddle.)

The residences on Water Street seen when entering Chestertown on State Route 213 North look much the same today. The Maryland State Roads Commission assumed ownership of this bridge in 1929. In 1930, nearly 5,000 people witnessed the opening of the new Chester River Bridge and its dedication as a memorial to the war veterans of Kent and Queen Anne's Counties. (Courtesy of William A. "Pat" Biddle.)

Gill Brothers Ice Cream Factory and Soda store, Fox's 5¢ to $1 Store, and the Chevrolet Dealership anchored Cross Street in downtown Chestertown for many years. Fox's relocated to open a larger store on High Street (which later became a McCrory's store), and the Chevrolet Dealership moved to a location on Route 213 North. The building has more recently been used for retail shops and offices. (Courtesy of William A. "Pat" Biddle.)

GILL BROS. RETAIL STORE AND FOUNTAIN LUNCH, CHESTERTOWN, MD.

This view shows High Street in downtown Chestertown looking west. Stam Hall, home of the Town Clock, is visible on the right, as is The Imperial Hotel. Stam Hall was built around 1886 for $15,000. Citizens of the town donated $800 toward the purchase and placement of the clock. The High Street streetscape looks much the same today as it did then. (Courtesy of William A. "Pat" Biddle.)

M. P. CHURCH, CHESTERTOWN, MD.

The Methodist Protestant Church, also known as Christ Methodist Church, is located on High Street in Chestertown. The church's lot was purchased for $3,150 in 1887. It is noted as an impressive brick Gothic Revival structure. An addition was added in recent years. Today the church has an active congregation. (Courtesy of William A. "Pat" Biddle.)

The Chestertown Post Office, built in 1935, is located on Spring Avenue in downtown Chestertown. Bibb's Inn was formerly located on this site before it was sold in the mid 1930s to the federal government specifically for a new post office. The first Chestertown postmaster was Marielene Lucas, who was appointed in 1899. Chestertown's post office was at one time located in Stam Hall. (Courtesy of William A. "Pat" Biddle.)

CHAPTER 2

Washington College

Washington College is a liberal arts co-ed college founded in 1782. Football began at Washington College in 1888 and the program lasted for 62 years. Today the school offers its students a variety of sports including baseball, softball, basketball, field hockey, lacrosse, rowing, sailing, swimming, tennis, and volleyball. (Courtesy of the Historical Society of Kent County.)

The Custom House, located on the Chester River in downtown Chestertown, is presently the home of Washington College's C. V. Starr Center for the Study of the American Experience. Built in 1746, it was the residence of Thomas Ringgold, a leader of the local Sons of Liberty. The restored building has original Georgian paneling, fireplaces, wide-board floors, and a riverfront porch. (Courtesy of the Historical Society of Kent County.)

Hodson Hall has served as the dining hall at Washington College for many years. The building, now known as Hodson Hall Commons, was renovated and expanded from 2009 to 2010. These two photographs show a contrast between then and now. In addition to the main dining room, today the building houses a student center, a performance area, a game room, and an office suite. (Courtesy of Karen Collier.)

The inside of Hodson Hall at Washington College is seen above in the 1950s, and below in 2010, when Hodson Hall Commons opened. The original Hodson Hall Building was a gift from the Clarence Hodson family. On the second floor, Hodson Hall Commons features a main dining room that offers a variety of seating areas, while the first floor boasts an innovative central entertainment and performance space, as well as café-style dining and a student center. (Courtesy of Karen Collier.)

In 1937, the building below was named the James W. Cain Gymnasium after former college president Dr. James W. Cain, who resigned in June of 1918. Dr. Cain succeeded Dr. Charles W. Reid as principal of Washington College. In 1968, Cain Gymnasium was demolished so the athletics facilities could be expanded. Those facilities were named the James W. Cain Athletic Center, as further tribute to Dr. Cain. A new library was built on the site of the former Cain Gymnasium. (Courtesy of the Historical Society of Kent County.)

This building on Washington Avenue in Chestertown, today known as Reid Hall, is part of the campus of Washington College. The building, which functions as a dormitory, was formerly known as Normal Hall when it was opened in 1897. In 1920, the name was changed to Charles W. Reid Hall in honor of Dr. Reid, who retired from his role as the principal of Washington College in 1903. (Courtesy of William A. "Pat" Biddle.)

The Frank Russell Gymnasium at Washington College opened in 1956. The Maryland General Assembly appropriated $250,000 for the new building. An addition was constructed and the building is now known as the Cain Athletic Center. Cain is home to men's and women's basketball, and women's volleyball. The facility also houses offices for physical education faculty, the director of athletics, coaches, sports information, locker rooms, and the Athletic Hall of Fame. (Courtesy of William A. "Pat" Biddle.)

The Hynson Ringgold House, located in Chestertown, overlooks the Chester River. Built by Thomas Ringgold in the early 1740s, it is known for its unusual antler staircase and hip roof. The house is listed on the National Register of Historic Places and has been the home of the presidents of Washington College since the late 1940s. (Courtesy of the Historical Society of Kent County.)

This building on the Washington College campus was at one time the college library. Bunting Library was a gift of Dr. George Avery Bunting, an 1891 graduate who went on to develop Noxema skin cream in 1914. Bunting Library existed until the opening of the Clifton M. Miller Library in 1971, built where Cain Gymnasium once stood. Bunting Library became Bunting Hall and now houses offices of the college administration. (Courtesy of William A. "Pat" Biddle.)

The Dr. H. A. B. Dunning Science Building on Washington College's campus opened in 1940. Dr. Dunning was a pharmaceutical chemist in Baltimore and a native of Caroline County on the Eastern Shore of Maryland. Dr. Dunning's support helped the College enlarge its facilities for teaching the sciences. The adjoining Alonzo G. Decker Jr. Laboratory Center opened in 1988, enabling Dunning Hall to be extensively renovated. In 2006 the Joseph H. McLain Atrium and the John S. Toll Science Center were constructed and, together with Dunning/Decker, make a state-of-the-art complex that houses classrooms, laboratories, and offices. (Courtesy of William A. "Pat" Biddle.)

CHAPTER 3

Rock Hall

At one time, Rock Hall, located on the Chesapeake Bay with easy access to the Chester River, Gray's Inn Creek, and Swan Creek, served as a main shipping point for seafood and agricultural products. Rock Hall is known today as a popular sailing and charter fishing boat center. (Courtesy of the Historical Society of Kent County.)

The Peoples Bank opened a Rock Hall branch in this location in 1921. The Peoples Bank of Chestertown, Maryland was established by an act of the General Assembly of Maryland on April 13, 1910. The original incorporators were William M. Slay, Dr. H. Benge Simmons, and L. Bates Russell. (Courtesy of H. Edward Beekman Jr.)

In 1916 , Rock Hall's Main Street boasted a bakery, two barbershops, a drugstore, a hotel, blacksmiths, a lumber yard, a livery stable, and two butchers. Today Main Street includes a grocery store, a real estate agency, The Mainstay (a performing arts venue), a drugstore and ice cream parlor, Java Rock coffeehouse, a dentist's office, and several gift shops. (Courtesy of H. Edward Beekman Jr.)

Rock Hall was established in 1707. Its location on the Chesapeake Bay contributed to it being the center of the Kent County oyster industry in 1916. George Washington and other men of note referred to the trip from Annapolis to Rock Hall on large schooners in their diaries. Rock Hall has served as the hub for commercial fishermen for many years, but as this industry has declined, recreational interests have taken hold. (Courtesy of H. Edward Beekman Jr.)

The Chesapeake Bay Bridge at Sandy Point, also referred to as the William Preston Lane Jr. Memorial Bridge, seen here from Rock Hall, opened to traffic on July 30, 1952, culminating a 45-year struggle. It is presently a dual-span bridge 4.3 miles in length. In 1973, a parallel span was added at a cost of $148 million. The bridge's two-lane original span (which today carries eastbound traffic) cost $45 million and was, at the time, the world's longest continuous over-water steel structure. (Courtesy of H. Edward Beekman Jr.)

The Citizens of Rock Hall erected the following marker in 1932: "Formerly known as Rock Hall Cross Roads, Main Street is part of the first road cut in Kent County in 1675. George Washington passed here eight known times. Tench Tilghman used this route from Yorktown to Philadelphia in October 1781." The crossroads remain today with the Rock Hall Methodist Church on one corner, a drugstore and ice cream parlor on one corner, and a coffeehouse and gift shop on the other corners. (Courtesy of the Historical Society of Kent County.)

In 2007, Rock Hall celebrated its 300th anniversary. The Rock Hall waterfront is home to both workboats and pleasure boats. Rock Hall is still known as a major fishing and oystering port on the upper Chesapeake Bay. Today the workboats are outnumbered by sailboats, while pleasure boats and fishing charters provide economic opportunities. Rock Hall is one of the larger sailing and charter boat fishing centers on the Eastern Shore. (Courtesy of H. Edward Beekman Jr.)

Wesley Chapel, located near Rock Hall, was established when Methodists in this area organized and decided to build a meetinghouse in 1829. The original meeting "chapel" was replaced in 1852 by the Greek Revival building that exists today. A cemetery adjoins the church. Once a year the church hosts a traditional Eastern Shore Fish Fry with the fish cooked over an open fire. (Courtesy of Judy Hickman.)

The Sharp Street wharf area of Rock Hall, located on the Chesapeake Bay, was transformed in the 1980s. Rock Hall Seafood was located where a popular spot for visitors, Waterman's Crabhouse, is today. The new "marina complex" was developed into Rock Hall Landing Marina, which features full-fingered floating docks, with 75 deepwater slips available for seasonal and transient berthing. (Courtesy of the Historical Society of Kent County.)

Durding's Store in Rock Hall has occupied the corner of Main and Sharp Streets for over 100 years. Today an authentic soda fountain and an old wooden telephone booth are of special interest to those visiting wishing to purchase ice cream, greeting cards, candies, gifts, and other items. (Courtesy H. Edward Beekman Jr.)

The former Rock Hall Fire Company Building was built in the 1950s. In addition to housing the town's fire fighting equipment, the upstairs "firehall" was often used for dances and dinners. It was sold in 2005, and the Rock Hall Volunteer Fire Company now occupies a new building on Route 20. The one-story building boasts a spacious room called "The Chesapeake Room," that is available for the community to rent. (Courtesy of Robin Kurowski.)

Mariner's Motel in Rock Hall overlooks the harbor and has been welcoming guests to the town for over 30 years. Rock Hall's history dates back 300 years. Generations of local watermen share its heritage as a major fishing, oystering, and crabbing port. Rock Hall's seafood business has declined over the years, but recreational boating and fishing are bringing new employment opportunities to the local residents today. (Courtesy of Robin Kurowski.)

CHAPTER 4

Other Kent County Areas

This wharf warehouse was located at Tolchester, near Rock Hall, in 1920. Tolchester Park has been developed into houses, and Tolchester Beach is now known as Tolchester Marina. Established in 1877, Tolchester was a popular Chesapeake Bay resort located on 155 acres, and served by six steamers and a ferry. It featured a hotel for guests, who could enjoy a dance hall, roller coaster, bowling alley, bingo parlor, boat rides, and many other amusements. It closed in 1962. (Courtesy of the Maryland Historical Society.)

This brick building is located in Millington and looks much the same as it did many years ago. It has been used as a firehouse with a community hall upstairs and also once served as a post office. Today it is used as a pharmacy. (Courtesy of the Historical Society of Kent County.)

Scheeler (Air) Field, formerly known as Gill Airport, was located on Route 213 north of Chestertown and remained open as the area's only airport until the early 1990s. The closing of Scheeler Field left the area with no public airport. (Courtesy of the Historical Society of Kent County.)

This building still houses the Still Pond Post Office in Still Pond, Maryland. Twelve years before the 19th Amendment established women's suffrage, Mary Jane Clark Howard, Anne Baker Maxwell, and Lillie Deringer Kelley cast their ballots in the municipal election of Still Pond in 1908. That year, an act for incorporation of the town had provided the right to vote to any male or female resident taxpayer over age 21. Fourteen women were registered to vote, two of them African American. (Courtesy of William A. "Pat" Biddle.)

Quaker Neck Landing is located on the Chester River a few miles from Chestertown. It serves today as a public landing for residents and for visitors. It is named for the Quaker movement, at one time prevalent in this area of Kent County. (Courtesy of Gwinn Derricott.)

This photograph of Kennedyville's main street was taken in the 1930s. Kennedyville, primarily residential in character, is said to be located in Kent County's agricultural heartland. The two-story building on the left continues to serve as the Kennedyville Post Office. The Kennedyville School, located on Main Street, operated for over 30 years before it was closed following a fire in 1949. A second school, constructed in 1949 to replace the closed school, shut its doors in the 1970s. (Courtesy of the Historical Society of Kent County.)

Built in 1712, Old St. Paul's Church, an 18th-century brick historic Episcopal church, is located near Fairlee in Kent. St. Paul's Parish, Kent, was one of the original 30 Anglican parishes in the Province of Maryland. It was listed on the National Register of Historic Places in 1980. (Courtesy of William A. "Pat" Biddle.)

Old St. Paul's Church, Kent Co., Md. (Built 1711)

The former Atlantic Hotel in Betterton is now an apartment building. The Town of Betterton was placed on the National Register of Historic Places in 1984. The Betterton Historic District consists of a collection of vernacular Victorian resort structures and includes many of the homes, hotels, and cottages built to accommodate steamboat passengers in the late 19th and early 20th centuries, dating from the golden age of the passenger steamboats on the Chesapeake Bay. (Courtesy of William A. "Pat" Biddle.)

This scenic view is a familiar sight at Betterton. In 1930, Betterton in Kent County was known as a summer resort, as well as for its year-round fishing industry. It is located at the mouth of the Sassafras River, overlooking the Chesapeake Bay at a point where five rivers empty into the Bay. As a summer resort, Betterton offered many sports. Hotels and boardinghouses accommodated guests. (Courtesy of the Maryland Historical Society.)

George Harper's store in Still Pond, Maryland, was built in the late 19th century, with additions constructed later. At the turn of the 20th century, Still Pond was a thriving community with a cannery and warehouse for produce from the surrounding farming area. The George Harper Store, operated by William Medders from 1894 to 1959, supplied the needs and luxuries of the citizenry of the area. A wooden boat shop and an art studio occupy the building today. (Courtesy of the Historical Society of Kent County.)

The "Worton Point Colored School No. 2" was built in 1890. This one-room schoolhouse served African-American students in grades one through six. It was last used as a school in 1958. It is now being restored as The African American Schoolhouse Museum and will house exhibits of photographs, artifacts, and oral histories of the lives and contributions of black families of early Kent County. (Courtesy of the Historical Society of Kent County.)

This bridge is located on Quaker Neck Road just outside of Chestertown. It spans Radcliffe Creek, now a popular creek for kayakers and canoers. It flows around the outskirts of Chestertown and continues past the Radcliffe Mill complex. (Courtesy of Gwinn Derricott.)

The Hotel Rigbie in Betterton offered its guests a most majestic view of the Sassafras River. The hotel, once overlooking the Chesapeake Bay, offered "resort accommodations of highest quality," with "running water in every room," and "meals that are master pieces." It was demolished and the Rigbie Bluff condos were constructed in its place. Betterton, settled by the Turner family, was a popular family resort for many years. It was a stopping place for the Philadelphia and Baltimore steamers. (Courtesy of William A. "Pat" Biddle.)

The Chester River Yacht and Country Club clubhouse opened in September 1928. It was reported that more than 400 automobiles were on the club grounds during the course of the evening dance, with many finding it necessary to park along the roadside. A golf tournament, as well as an exhibition golf match and tennis tournament, were among the day's activities. The original nine-hole golf course was designed by Alexander H. Findlay. (Courtesy of the Historical Society of Kent County.)

The Methodist Church

Kennedyville, Maryland

Edward J. Bond, D. D., Minister

Mrs. William E. Anthony . . . . Organist

"I was glad when they said unto me, Let us go into the house of the Lord." Psalm 122:1

The Kennedyville United Methodist Church is located in Kennedyville, Maryland. The church celebrated its 150-year anniversary in 2010. It was originally known as Waters Chapel and was named after Rev. Francis Waters, who served as president of the Maryland Methodist Protestant Conference from 1842 to 1846 and again from 1862 to 1866. Reverend Waters also served as president of Washington College in Chestertown from 1818 to 1823 and from 1854 to 1860. (Courtesy of Mary Anna Gustafson.)

Godlington Manor was listed on the National Register of Historic Places in 1972. The "Manor of Godlington" was originally 1,000 acres and was patented to Thomas Godlington, a London merchant, in 1659 with Court Baron only. Michael Miller acquired the property in 1686 and his heirs retain ownership of the Manor House and lands to this day. (Courtesy of the Historical Society of Kent County.)

In 1946, the late James T. Ozman opened Ozman's Body Shop. It was primarily a place that repaired and rebuilt wrecked automobiles. The business, later known as Ozman's Inc., grew and included new car franchises for Pontiacs, Oldsmobiles, GMC Trucks, and Jeeps. The company changed hands in the early 1970s, and now Ozman's grandson operates the business, renamed Todd's, and continues repairing and rebuilding damaged cars, as well as selling used cars. (Courtesy of Patricia Joan O. Horsey.)

The Most Precious Blood Catholic Church building is located in Betterton. Construction of the church began in 1916 and the Rev. James P. Fitzgerald is said to have built much of the church himself. It was occupied until 1994. The Town of Betterton purchased the property in 2006 at a cost of $395,000 and is currently using grant funding to renovate the building to be used as a community building. (Courtesy of the Horsey Collection.)

Owen Cottage and Annex in Betterton offered overnight accommodations to many visitors over the years. These buildings were known in the early 1930s as the Maplewood Manor and Maplewood Annex. Both buildings remain today and are privately owned. Betterton flourished at the beginning of the 20th century as a resort town. Originally known as Crew's Landing, this former fishing village was renamed after Elizabeth Betterton, the wife of Richard T. Turner, who bought "Fish Hall" and the Palmer Farm in 1850. Turner then went on to build Ellwood, which still stands on the southern edge of town, facing Howell Point Road. (Courtesy of the Horsey Collection.)

Betterton once was home to a number of Victorian hotels and guesthouses. Visitors enjoyed the beach and the many activities available. The influx of out-of-towners decreased with the decline of steamboat traffic. Betterton today boasts a 5-acre waterfront park and is one of two public beaches in Kent County on the Chesapeake Bay. (Courtesy of the Historical Society of Kent County.)

Mears Great Oak Landing Resort Marina is located a few miles from Chestertown on Fairlee Creek just off of the Chesapeake Bay. "Great Oak Lodge" began in 1955 as a private yacht club and marina. Today it is a 70-acre resort marina that includes, among other amenities, a restaurant, a 28-room lodge, banquet facilities, and a swimming pool. (Courtesy of the Horsey Collection.)

WEER'S HALL, Kennedyville, Md.

Weer's Hall, Kennedyville, was built in 1906 by Joseph H. Weer for use as a store, post office, and telephone office. There was a public hall on the second floor. It was later owned and operated by the Youngs, who lived in an apartment on the second floor. In recent years the building has been used as a gift shop, rug shop, and antique shop.

The Tolchester Beach Amusement Park bathing beach, located on the Chesapeake Bay, is now part of the Tolchester Marina. The remaining acreage of the "Park" was developed for housing. The Tolchester Steamboat Company opened Tolchester Beach Amusement Park, which grew to over 150 acres and included a hotel, pavilion, bathing beach, and a variety of rides and attractions. The Park closed in 1962. (Courtesy of the Historical Society of Kent County.)

The Kitty Knight House, located on the Kent County side of Georgetown, is named for Miss Catherine "Kitty" Knight (1775–1855), an early American heroine credited with saving part of Georgetown during the War of 1812. Georgetown was founded in 1736. Today the Kitty Knight House offers lodging and a restaurant. (Courtesy of the Historical Society of Kent County.)

Bailey's Hotel, facing Sassafras Street at the crossroads in Millington, was built to replace the previous hotel that burned in the great fire of 1904. The hotel thrived during its early years, mainly due to the patronage of the many traveling salesmen arriving on the train to promote their wares to local businesses. The building is used as apartments today. (Courtesy of the Historical Society of Kent County.)

About the Authors

R. Jerry Keiser earned a B.A. in history from Salisbury University, Maryland, and an M.L.S. in Library Science from Catholic University of America. He is presently the librarian at the Kent County Public Library in Chestertown, Maryland. He serves on the Maryland Advisory Board of the National Historical Publications and Records Commission.

Patricia Joan O. Horsey is a native of Kent County. She received a B.S. in urban studies from the University of Maryland. She operated two retail businesses in downtown Chestertown for many years, served as a judicial officer for the state of Maryland, and is currently a real estate salesperson. Horsey is a member of the Old Kent Chapter of the Daughters of the American Revolution and the Kitty Knight Chapter of the National Society of the United States Daughters of 1812. She has an interest in local history and genealogy and is a member of the Historical Society of Kent County, the Upper Shore Genealogical Society, and the National Genealogical Society. She serves on the board of directors of the Chestertown Library Inc., the Foundation for the Kent County Public Library, and The Peoples Bank of Kent County. Horsey has an interest in antiques and is a current member of the Choptank Chapter of the American Antique Arts Association and the Cadwalader of Kent Questers. She is very interested in the accurate reporting of local history and in providing a permanent repository for significant historical information.

William A. "Pat" Biddle, a Kent County native, began collecting post cards at a very early age. What began as childhood entertainment became a lifelong hobby. He particularly enjoys creating shadowboxes with post cards in the background and figures dressed in period costumes that illustrate the history of the Eastern Shore including Tolchester and Betterton resorts that flourished in the 1920s and 1930s. Pat holds a master's degree in education from Western Maryland College. He retired a few years ago after a long career as an educator and is currently a member of the Barbershop Society and sings with the local barbershop chapter.

Index

www.arcadiapublishing.com

Discover books about the town where you grew up, the cities where your friends and families live, the town where your parents met, or even that retirement spot you've been dreaming about. Our Web site provides history lovers with exclusive deals, advanced notification about new titles, e-mail alerts of author events, and much more.

MADE IN THE USA

Arcadia Publishing, the leading local history publisher in the United States, is committed to making history accessible and meaningful through publishing books that celebrate and preserve the heritage of America's people and places. Consistent with our mission to preserve history on a local level, this book was printed in South Carolina on American-made paper and manufactured entirely in the United States.

This book carries the accredited Forest Stewardship Council (FSC) label and is printed on 100 percent FSC-certified paper. Products carrying the FSC label are independently certified to assure consumers that they come from forests that are managed to meet the social, economic, and ecological needs of present and future generations.

FSC
Mixed Sources
Product group from well-managed forests and other controlled sources

Cert no. SW-COC-001530
www.fsc.org
© 1996 Forest Stewardship Council

Find Your Place in History.